ON THIS SIDE O

On This Side of the Desert

Poems by

Alfredo Aguilar

The Kent State University Press

Kent, Ohio

The Wick Poetry Series is sponsored by the Stan and Tom Wick Poetry Center and the Department of English at Kent State University.

Cataloging information for this title is available at the Library of Congress.

24 23 22 21 20   5 4 3 2 1

CONTENTS

Indigenous relationships to land have always been dangerous to the Americas. The intimacy we have with this land—that our bodies, languages, stories, and dreams are made of its clay and waters and seeds and thorns—has been weaponized by governments across the globe. *On This Side of the Desert* allows the desert to become or recognizes what it has always been, a body like any other, both winning and losing, wounded with desire and scarred with memory, tethered to where it has been and reaching toward what it thirsts for. From the book's first poem, "I Woke Up in the Wilderness," Aguilar makes clear the stakes wagered in his Borderlands pastorals, where the speaker is in a perpetual a battle with, against, and even for the desert and the lives it has given or taken from us and has yet to give or take from us. Aguilar writes:

> . . . i picked a fallen feather
> off the ground & let it dangle from my ear. i ate
>
> a cactus pear—spat out a thimble of silver. the saguaro
> *told me you can learn to live on the smallest giving—*
>
> *to hold a palm full of water & make it last a season.*

To make a border of any land is to attempt to alter our bodies and our tongues, to sever us from our roots so that we don't bloom into our futures. Aguilar's poems challenge our spatial ideas of what the borderlands are, as well as the way time works or does not work under the imposed conditions of a border. The Borderland in these poems is reshuffled and remapped, as a place of haunting and responsibility, yet also a place of desire and fruiting. This desert, and the crossing itself, in many ways, become the center instead of the edge or fringes, until we lose track of which side is the right side and the wrong side, which side we left, and which we arrived in. Aguilar asks again and again in these poems what does it mean to cross—a border, a page, a story, a heartbreak, or a hope—and are we ever allowed to stop crossing? In the title poem of the book, he builds a heartbreaking condition of a desert and its natural and unnatural cycles of blooming and dying:

nests of gila woodpeckers

poke their heads out
of a saguaro. i look

at their curious eyes.
raul, i say & the saguaro

blooms. i stare back
at the flood. i say

my mother's name,
cristina & desert marigolds

crack through a boulder.
i say my father's name, *martin*

& all the novena candles
in the bed of the truck are aglow.

i say *santos* & in a pair
of footprints in the sand

a man is built up
from the part of his body

that most touched
this earth.

Yes, the crossing both fruits in the heart and haunts in the mind. When this event is a part of your ancestry and inheritance, how do we meet it again and again each day? How do we meet ourselves, even? Is it possible to ever leave the imagination of our childhoods, where many of our first wounds were earned, and is it a luck or a penance to know the pathway back to those wounds so well? Aguilar wrestles with these questions in the many poems of family history and legacy, retelling tales from the perspective of a boy. Our young speaker is given an incredible generosity and is allowed to hold both love and fear, both tenderness and pain, as he recounts his connections to family as well as his own coming of age, as a poet, as a man, as someone still becoming.

If it's true what they say, that our futures are made of our pasts, perhaps we are always walking backward toward everything that is possible. Aguilar's work asks: Not only what but whom does the poet risk when they set their *recuerdos* onto the tables of any electricity-haunted night or terribly sunlit afternoon of writing to tell a story about what has happened in order to leap toward what has yet to happen? Aguilar is risking at least a family, and language, and a terrible, beautiful desert of beloveds and strangers. Most importantly, and as he writes in his final poem of the collection, "Origin Myth," Aguilar is risking rising into every morning, as light.

. . . the child so desperate
to be near those far away reached into the sky & became

smoke. the child who continued to love unbittered
by this world became the sun. he rises every morning to cover

the earth in light & look how he has never dimmed.

ACKNOWLEDGMENTS

I am immensely grateful to the readers & editors at the following venues in which these poems first appeared, at times in earlier versions:

92 Y Unterberg Poetry Center—My Mother Drove Us into Tijuana for Dentistry
The Adroit Journal—Borrando la Frontera
BOAAT Journal—After Three Beers My Tia Talks about the Border
The Boiler—I Woke Up in the Wilderness
Cosmonauts Avenue—In Boyhood; Tonight Your Mother is Running with Coyotes
The Journal—Yellow House
Maps for Teeth—Mexico-Tenochtitlan
Redivider—My Father Makes Me Hold a Hen
Salt Hill Journal—Childhood is a Realm
The Shallow Ends—Origin Myth
Tinderbox Poetry Journal—As a Child I Watch My Mother Sit in Limbo; The Monsters My Parents Warned Me about Speak in Their Defense; Mamá Chelo Stands at the Concrete Washboard
Wildness—The Boy Considers Being Born Elsewhere; Through the Reeds
Winter Tangerine—On This Side of the Desert
Vinyl Poetry & Prose—On a Ranch My Father Broke Horses

There are so many people who have contributed to this book, these poems. This book would not be what it is without my friends who are foundational to my understanding of what poetry can be & sound & look like.

I'm forever grateful to the following people for their generosity & friendship while making art alongside one another other—Hari Alluri, Cheyenne Bartram, Charlie Beaz, Chestina Craig, Mario Di Mateo, Sophia Farmer, Jacob Jones, Shannon Linzer, Joe Limer, Mark Maza, Sheila Sadr & Zane Timpson.

I want to give a special thank you to Rolland Tizuela for creating Glassless Minds, the open mic where so many of these friendships formed & my earliest poems blossomed.

I am indebted to the various poetry communities in & around San

Diego & Los Angeles—I've learned so much from sharing my words with others & listening to others share their words.

Many thanks to the following spaces for carving out a place to create art & for the friendships & guidance I found there: The Bread Loaf Writer's Conference, The Frost Place, The MacDowell Colony, The Speakeasy Project, The Vermont Studio Center, VONA Writer's Workshop & Winter Tangerine's Summer Workshop.

Immense gratitude to Karla Cordero, always an early reader & the person who told me I had a book when I wasn't sure if I did.

Mil gracias to Natalie Diaz for her generous advice, for seeing these poems & believing in them. Wild gratitude to the Wick Poetry Center & Kent State University Press for making this book a reality.

To my beloved Laura Villareal, for your light & support—for being my partner in everything.

To my family—Cristina, Martin, Alex & Gemma, for your kindness & joy—for showing me all the forms love takes.

& lastly to you reader, for taking time to sit with these words.

I WOKE UP IN THE WILDERNESS

& could not tell what time it was. i walked
beside you in the dark & you became

a white owl. you flew onto a mesquite branch, turned
your head, opened your small noble beak,

looked into me, then flew away. i picked a fallen feather
off the ground & let it dangle from my ear. i ate

a cactus pear—spat out a thimble of silver. the saguaro
told me *you can learn to live on the smallest giving—*

to hold a palm full of water & make it last a season.
i looked up & the clouds on the moon shivered.

i spoke with a coyote. he told me how the world
was born—*in the beginning,* he said, *an ocean.*

he licked my palms clean. told me *i howl only*
to try & call back everything that has left me.

the first thing i learned
was silence & the promise
of its safety. i was born
only because my parents
had crossed unseen
into the country—
lead north
underneath a dim sky.
where streets were in
their language. where they
were thought not to speak.
were only wanted
for their muscle. made
sure their feet left
no marks in the ground.
that their bodies
did not cast
a shadow. or else
la migra finds you &
sends you back.
& a friend of theirs
who was too loud
or not careful enough
or just unlucky
did not come home
for nights & his children
never stopped asking
where he went.
my uncles tell me
that before i was born
my father
hardly ever spoke. during
a parent-teacher conference
mrs. garrison tells
my mother that i give
her no trouble.

that i am so quiet.
that i don't even wear
colors that shout.

but because you are a child
you do not know this. you tug
on your father's jeans, look
up at him & ask *where is amá?*
he looks at you, but says
nothing. he cannot tell you
that she is traveling through
an arid night, past mountains,
sagebrush & metal-wrought
fence back to you. instead, he
distracts you with television.
before going to sleep, you look
through a window into the
night & notice how the sky
carries less light. tonight both
the moon & your mother are
missing.

raul & i drive by a yellow sign
that reads *cuidado—no exponga*

*su vida a los elementos—no vale
la pena.* we pass a mountain

where, tucked away in a place
that the relentless sun

cannot reach, the direction
& miles left to the border

are scratched into a boulder.
raul tells me that yesterday,

under a creosote bush, he found
a knapsack holding only

a lightbulb & a battered bible.
the body nearby, so far from god.

the legs consumed by cramps.
the skin wrung of its sweat.

all the water escaping
the body to try & keep

it cool. the clothes stitched
onto his skin by the sun.

last night's full moon
a final eucharist his mouth

could not reach. he had
a name—santos. he also had

a wife. or maybe it was a mother,
or a sister, or a daughter.

the wallet didn't say.
we stop at a white crucifix

staked into the ground
where there are no roads

& leave twelve bottles
of water & twelve pears.

raul tells me
that he once found

an entire skeleton
in torn clothes,

the sneakers still tied
to its feet. on our way back

to the otro lado a flash
flood rushes across

the road in front us. we stop,
step out & face it. we leave

the truck running,
the speakers aching

y volver, volver. sweat collects
at the base of the gold

crucifix necklace underneath
my shirt. *the rains are short*

but so heavy, i say. *right, raul?*
nests of gila woodpeckers

poke their heads out
of a saguaro. i look

at their curious eyes.
raul, i say & the saguaro

blooms. i stare back
at the flood. i say

my mother's name,
cristina & desert marigolds

crack through a boulder.
i say my father's name, *martin*

& all the novena candles
in the bed of the truck are aglow.

i say *santos* & in a pair
of footprints in the sand

a man is built up
from the part of his body

that most touched
this earth. i say the names

of my tías, tíos, primos
& a bronzed mass

dressed in white rises
from the rushing flood.

their backs are turned
to me—they wear

my family's shoulders.
they head north. before them

the white obelisk marking
the line in the ground

crumbles. before them
every metal fence parts.

found discipline at the end
of a whip. punished the wild
colt for disobedience. it threw
its body on him, flailed

& left him covered in a new coat
of dust. used rope to force
the colt to kneel before him & it never
again tried to jump. my father

was shaped by hands that were
fatherless. withheld a warmth
they did not know how to offer. his own hands
grew thick with calluses. he learned

bury, learned stone face & called them
strength. the night his mother
passed his voice was a quiet swell. a rope
loosened & an unbridled sorrow bucked

against the walls of his throat. it rose
on its hind legs, nostrils flared. he bit
his lip, felt the pull of a metal bar
along his tongue & did not weep.

AFTER THREE BEERS MY TÍA TALKS ABOUT THE BORDER

en aquel tiempo we would wait for night to fall
& then cross from tijuana easily. there was hardly any migra

then. not like now. today there's a chingo de migra
all the way up to san ysidro & past that. they got vans

& guns & dogs—you've seen it. it's not like before.
then gente started coming through the desert & algunos

don't make it out, sabes? sometimes familias don't ever know
what happens to the bodies. their names stop blooming

in their family's throats & the family lights a candle for an empty
casket. it's not safe, even with coyotes. you can't always trust

them. una vez i heard that after they paid him, the coyote left
behind the gente he was bringing over in the middle of desert.

te imaginas? shit, if you're already here you don't want to visit
home & then risk your life coming back. your primito

probably wouldn't recognize my face i've been away
so long. he's grown up so fast. está así de alto. sabes,

he once told me *mami, i'm going to cross the desert*
or find a tunnel & join you. i told him *ni se te ocurra esa*

estupidez. it's sweet, but i'll bring him over after
i get my papels sorted. no chingues, the first time i crossed

i crawled under a fence. my stomach was covered
with dirt. stars were out. i don't know if i ever rose.

MY MOTHER DROVE US INTO TIJUANA FOR DENTISTRY

because we didn't have
american health insurance.
past otay mesa checkpoint
were billboards in spanish
& narrow rutted streets.

on our left were rows of cars
waiting to enter the u.s.—

our dentist, ignacio, was a friend
from my mother's childhood & often
they'd reminisce about their small town.
folks they knew, folks that had passed—
how the town looked so different now—
how their lives led them here,
with my mother leaving the country.

i sat in a dental chair & ignacio mixed putty
until it was pink. he needed an impression
of my top teeth for retainers. i tasted
a cold metal tray that kept the mold
in place. after a minute he unwedged it
& my mouth smacked of chalk. before leaving
my mother asked ignacio about
a new denture—the one she had was old.
until that moment i never knew
my mother had false teeth.

in our car, in the middle
of an expanse of cars
waiting to get back into the u.s.
my mother said *i lost a lot*
of my teeth when i was young.
she removed her top denture—
smiled at me, revealed a dark gap

between rows of ivory.
she tried to say something &
it came out jumbled. she laughed,
not covering the gap,
then i laughed with all my teeth
& she pushed hers back into her mouth—
i've worn these for a long time.
i don't want that for you.

from the window
i watched older men
push carts between
stopped cars. they sold balloons,
bright popsicles, aguas, dulces.
a currency exchange booth
announced all i could buy
with just one american dollar.
i looked at my mother—
noticed her denture
yellowing at its edges
& saw her without it.

my mother left—
came to america—
had crossed for this.

IN THE SECOND MONTH

the officers whose sole job
it was to make people vanish
grew into visibility. the people
who had always lived
in a quiet panic
watched the room
they were in slowly fill
with smoke—
it reached the ceiling,
curled & rested
in their hair.
more eyes watched now.
some dreaded a knock
on the door
would seize them.

on the radio,
a business owner spoke
about selling all
she built—
for fear that soon
she would be taken
out of the country.
she made her children
citizens of her first nation—
would bring them over
if she was removed.

the person in the house
across the street
who tended
to the rose gardens
every day
disappeared
& bushels of pink
rose petals

lay wrecked
in the dirt.

my mother
sent me a picture
she had taken
of an officer
in a supermarket—
strapped & armed.
can you believe this?
she asked.

i heard
they stood
outside courthouses
like birds of prey
whose cries mimicked
the sound of boots
on pavement.

i saw more
of their metal boxcars
on the road.
while driving past one
my muscles locked—
the vehicle parked
like a crouched panther—
its sharp yellow eyes
watching for the vulnerable
in a crowd.
the quick worried glance.
the sweat on temples.
anything suspect & leapt.

i had no reason
to be afraid—

but i grew up
in the shadow
of my parents' fear.

when i was younger
& my tía alicia would visit
we would drive
on the nearby roads
to check if la migra
were at their posts.
seeing nothing,
we would call
to tell her it was safe.
none of this
seemed strange to us—

who wouldn't do this
for their family?

in 2012, artist ana teresa fernández painted part of the
u.s./méxico border to give the wall the illusion of
transparency.

i watched her dip/bristles in blue paint/she coated the red-brown metal
fence/rendered transparent/the thing that separated her from her son/the
wound caked over with blue/opposite her/a woman in a green uniform/
made what she guarded invisible/the wall disappeared/the sky pulled
down over rust/this is how a new north sky was built/the first cloud that
passed through it took the shape/of a beloved's face whose eyes i had
forgotten/a child unspooled white thread & the wind picked up her red
kite/suspended it in the blue/a second sun appeared/a bedraggled heart
beating with hurt/it set in the north along the new horizon/turned the
blue to pink rose/to violet softening/the underbellies of clouds/at night
i looked up/at the new stars/named each one after a person/i could not
hold/mapped constellations/named them home familia/all their memory
burning/all their light stretching toward me/on this side of the sky

MY MOTHER SAYS HER CHILDHOOD HOME IS HAUNTED

& that one night, she overheard
the frantic stomp of horse hooves

coming from the backyard. concerned
they would escape, she warned

her father. when he went out
to see, he saw only the horses

upright in their sleep, dreaming—
but noticed each of their manes

had been braided by some phantom hand.
another time, her small dog stood

on the rooftop barking then quickly went silent—
she could only hear the wind whistling.

the dog disappeared & a week later
returned in a man's arms—he found him

in brush, trembling. the dog was thin & cowered
as though it had fought something & lost.

at the end of that week his heart stopped.
one evening, she & her family

were outside talking with neighbors,
when they heard a lone flute singing

from inside their empty house. they looked
at one another & my mother ran back inside

to find no one & her flute
locked away in its case. she tells me

she never drinks water before going to bed—
i ask why. she looks at me, says

i don't want to get up in the dark, walk
to the bathroom & have something find me.

WHEN LA MIGRA CAUGHT MY FATHER

the first time, he was young—still without
a family of his own. the white border patrol agent

clad in green drove my father back
to the border & knowing he would try again,

the way everyone does, told him *it's your job
to try to get in & it's our job to try & keep you out.*

shrunk need to a game—my father the mouse,
the country a clawed cat. a cartoon drama

for a cartoon hunger. shrunk policing
the boundary of a bejeweled empire

to sweeping the streets in the nice part of town
that never questions how it gained its wealth.

where immaculate yards, roads & cars
make poor strangers unwelcome—

says, *we want the uncouth kept*
                                        out.

my small fingers curl around a cow's teat. i point
it in the direction of the pail below. i don't want to harm
the cow & tug gently. i look up at my father wondering why

there isn't any milk & he laughs. says, *no hubieran aguantado vivir
aquí.* he crouches, places his callused hands on the base
of two teats & tugs. milk shoots out, hisses as it fills the pail.

a tail of steam rises from the top. in the house where my father
was raised, we drink milk meant for the mouth of a calf.
we sit at a table where a thin layer of plastic protects

the white lace beneath. outside chickens run across the yard.
a bag of maíz sits in a shed. there are no video games
& the only television set in the house has knobs. *life here*

is very different from the way you've grown up, my father says.
i think what he means is that he was born into work
& i was born into a crib. that he is one of fifteen sets of teeth.

that he quit his schooling to cut crops. that he lied
about his age when trying to find work in the u.s.—
said he was eighteen when he was only sixteen.

i don't know who my father is without sweat.
without his rough fingers, his mustache.
i have never seen a single photograph of him as a boy.

AS A CHILD I WATCH MY MOTHER
SIT IN LIMBO

with other strangers
who stepped out of their shadows
for papers. placed there

by a begrudging state
that claims fairness—
a tiny flame gnaws at the border

of my mother's dress.
she puts it out with her palm.
here they take her

fingerprints & document
the shape of her hands.
one day, at the front desk

a lady tells her
i am sorry missus,
but your paperwork was lost

in the mouth of a whirlwind.
we'll have to restart your application—
& my mother sits inside

that somber room
for another two years.
on the wall

a portrait of the president
looks over everyone.
my mother's stay is provisional

but she is nervous
about how law can be read
& carried out.

how under different eyes
her steps on the soil
    become a question.

    she sits stiff
in a foreign plastic chair.
    unable to swim back across

    a rusted river pushing
two bodies away
    from one another.

    i am from here,
but my mother
    is my first home.

    i've learned to hold
everything as though
    it can be taken.

MÉXICO-TENOCHTITLÁN

i walk through a city built atop a lake—dirt & asphalt
packed underneath my feet. i return to the violent origin
that birthed the story of my skin, its contempt for itself—
after its siege the spaniards leveled the temples
& then called them ruins. constructed new houses
atop the old. gave the city a different name. poured
dust into canals that carried boats. today the clay
is drying—thirst sinks buildings closer to the dead
lake below—an open wound large enough to swallow
a new faith. i walk past an ancient chapel
slumped into the ground, on its knees & praying,
its bells ringing out the hour. everything in this city
was called something else once & it can't forget.
the past is never past. it is a gash that does not close.
that continues to shape my face. that i build on & out of
while below a hundred hands draw me in by my name.

THE BOY CONSIDERS BEING BORN ELSEWHERE

he is born & raised on the land his grandfather
cared for. one morning he wakes & is in a different
country. neighbors lose land that generations have
been buried in. the white american squatters claim
the land for themselves & do not leave. they believe
everything they touch does not have a history.
he tells them to leave. they bludgeon him & hang
him on the tree his grandfather tended to as a child.

//

he is born in a town in the northeast of the country
& is raised by his tía. he knows the embrace of his
parents best when wrapping his small tongue around
the syllables in their names. here the sun hides
for a season. at school he is the only brown child in class.
he points to a photograph when asked where his
parents are. he says, *once, i gave the night all my tears
& i haven't seen my father since.* he gazes at the sky
expecting an answer.

//

he is born in the town where his parents are from.
he devotes himself to god, marries, has children.
watches the town become dry & cracked, but cannot
leave. his children head north. a different life miles
away—highways wide as rivers. days in the desert,
they say. packed like sardines, they say. he hears
their voices through a telephone wire. they send
money back. his youngest, eduardo, left in spring—
he was never heard from again.

//

he is born in the town where his father is from.
sus padres se van para el otro lado & he is raised by
his abuelos. his parents send money back. every
school year he gets new clothes. he believes his
parents are something that only the rain can bring.
he prays for floods. he imagines america is on
the other side of the mountain range. he tells his
abuelos when he is old enough he will climb those
mountains to join his parents—his legs will carry
him.

that language charts like any map. *do you remember—*
as an infant, your mother bathed you in sugar

water. your father, having returned from work, lifted
you up & you kissed his warm stubbled cheek, then winced

because he tasted like the ocean. here, your parents
were only ever parents. you sat in the backseat singing

along to a cassette tape, throwing syllables like fistfuls
of rice. you placed a popsicle inside the microwave—

said it was too cold. in the garage you, your little brother
& cousin chanted around a poisonous snake your father

had severed with an axe. you plucked a pomegranate off
the neighbor's tree & opened it with a bat—your fingers,

teeth & t-shirt stained sticky purple-red. on picture day,
it was so warm you took off the buttoned shirt your mother

chose just for you & posed grinning in a white tank top.
you danced home from the hospital with your new-

born sister, whose name you had won in a coin toss. during
a game of hide & seek, your mother whispered, *hide where we leave*

the clothes & you hid inside the dryer. you lay in that dark
curved belly, refused to come out when everyone called

your name & no one ever found you—

THE FIRST TIME I WENT TO THE CINEMA

i stepped inside a dim theater room. the aisle lit
like a runway. i wanted to run down it—

my small arms open wide. to fly through the air &
be weightless. my little brother picked a row

to sit in & we were small for the cushion seats.
my sneakers dangled above the floor.

dark filled the room & a small point
of light spread into color before us.

like watching a full moon—it felt private.
even while viewing with the rest of the world.

sound swelled from the walls
& i felt the frames begin to shake.

i covered my ears
to keep the world from bursting.

the glow from behind me
gave way to a landscape on the screen

& i was not where i was sitting.
the tiny point of light unrolled

an entire savanna before my eyes.
a purple sun rose & animals leapt out

of a stream. in the movie, before the small lion
lost his father in a stampede, he looked down

to see a pair of rocks trembling. & i, too, small
& with a father, feet hung above the ground

looked to the floor thinking the dark would shake.

THE MONSTERS MY PARENTS WARNED
ME ABOUT SPEAK IN THEIR DEFENSE

i. el coco

without shape,
                                i take a child. cloak myself in
        the shadow of a room. look through
                        an iron pan with holes. façade for a face,
a candle wick burning behind it. i want to
                        tend to a thing, watch it grow & hear it say
        i love you back. to run my hand along
                        their soft cheek—a caress. wipe tears from
their eyes. tell my child *te quiero,*
                kiss their forehead
                                        & lift them away.

ii. chupacabra

i undress
the warmth
in the body

draw all
the red out
of flesh &

am called
abomination
in moonlight

i watch
tended herds
& christen

each creature's
tender neck
before breaking

the body gone
slack i empty
its veins

i bless it
with smoke i utter
a prayer *oh lord*

spare me
for taking a life
to preserve

my own

iii. la llorona

& see what i would do for love? submerge
the likeness of us until it no longer breathes.
devote myself to my own drowning. let my hair
become a trail of smoke underneath the water.
cry out beside a river until it is a lullaby. the river-
bed a cradle i lower all the children into.
mis hijos, perdóname. every face looks like yours.

against the dirt. i feel its plumage,
panic as it struggles to get out

of my grasp. he yells at me
con ganas! como si tienes huevos!

   & lightning flashes
through me. i want to shove him,

but i do nothing, say nothing—
just clench the bird's wings tighter

as he brings a knife down on its neck.
   once, my father looked at me

& said *i don't know what's to become
of you* & i think he meant

i was never who he expected—
in turn, i learned he was someone

i could never expect to be more
   than missing—a man who bartered

a pitted love in tasks. he once hid
my pair of tight-fitting jeans

while they were drying
on the clothesline because

   en esta casa, no quiero un maricón.
in my adolescent school gloom,

he wanted to seize all my
songs—my small compasses—

because he believed they were
the blue root of my sorrow.

    blood from the hen's neck colors
the dirt murky brown. the hen twitches

in my grip, then goes limp. i loosen
my grasp—each palm damp with sweat.

the hen's marbled pupil,
looks up at my father & i—

reflecting what we've done
with each other

        using only our hands.

AVOWAL

everyone i've ever loved split me
open & fed me a warm meal
after. i was a shell of lime filled
with coconut & sugar, cherished
on another's tongue.
i retreated into my mirror
& everyone i cared for vanished
from their portraits.
i carried my mother's face,
my father's distance. i tried
to find a language on my loaned skin
& make it mine—
find me
etching letters into the dirt
attempting, again & again,
to build a home.

FAMILY HISTORY

time is a hall of mirrors reflecting
the movement of a palm at once
& onward. my great-

> grandfather vanished into
> his own hands & left
> his family behind.

my grandfather's touch was distant—
busied himself in fields & livestock
for the sake of family—taught
his children to do the same.

> my father spent evenings after work
> alone in his shop hammering hot metal
> to his will, while my mother stood
> left of zero.

i spend my time behind a closed
door bent over a desk pounding shapes
into speech. or over a hollow wooden
instrument bending myself to fit
inside of a column of air.

> when wearing a hat my mother says
> i look so much like my father.
> my brother wears his pelo rizado,
> his curls. my sister wears
> his silence.

between every child & parent
is the length of a country,
but how far can a child stray from
the hands their parents gave them,
the roads carved into their palms—

I RETURNED TO THE ALTAR

& could not recognize it. the light swallowed,
the statues' faces worn away, the ofrendas rotted. i knelt

& could not fit inside my own prayer. the walls pushed
me out—the sky shook. i rushed down a flight

of stone steps & did not stop. i ran with a herd of bison—
their soft brown coats lifted clouds of earth onto my skin.

they fell away & i was the only thing left hurtling into
the night. i spent weeks chasing suns. i abandoned

my name & stopped in field of cleared oaks. on a stump
every person that had ever pulled me through their mouth

was stacked in a ring, one atop the other. i wanted to be
forgiven, to be absolved of memory—to skin the shadows

it cast. i tore out my own heart—wet red clay dripping
in my palm—& cast it off a cliff. something smaller grew

in its place—inside, a green hummingbird thrashed.

PASSING

       i awake to my mother on the phone
i hear her break   she cries into the receiver
      i hear it all   last week she bought a ticket
to return home   to care for her ill mother

      i hear her   break into the receiver
qué   *cómo paso*   *se que no estaba bien pero*
    unable to return   to care for her mother
on the night before   the plane would take her home

      qué   *cómo paso*   *se que no estaba bien pero*
skin drained of color   a growth in the body
    on the night before   the plane would take her home
i watch my mother learn   how to not have a mother

     skin drained of color   a growth in the body
i awake to my mother on the phone
     i watch my mother learn   how to lose her mother
i saw it all   last week she bought a ticket

my mother left   the country for three months
to lay her mother   & her grief inside a box
          in those months   my father did not call or visit her

          one night after she returned   i was in the bathroom
heard my parents'   faint voices through the wall
i pressed   my ear against their door   they were arguing
          they were planning to separate   i sank & couldn't move
they opened the door   found me   made me swear
not to tell my younger brother & sister what i heard

          my father began sleeping outside in a trailer
no one asked why   my father wanted to keep my mother
          or his idea of her   the idea of his family
pero era demasiado tarde   she told me
          she felt for so long   they lived their lives
in separate rooms   she brought us to school
          to soccer practice   to birthday parties
                    always alone

after my sister graduated   my parents sat my siblings down
          said they were separating   that year my mother left
the house she raised us in   my father axed the tree
whose branches were entwined   with the passion fruit vine
          stopped speaking to my mother altogether
started using his children as couriers   during christmas
my mother gifted me a card   *i'm sorry*
if i've cause you any pain   este año no hacido fácil pero
          we still have   each other   i love you so much
that year passed like any other   we could do nothing
                    to turn it back

on my way home   i looked toward the mountains
          the ones that stood over my childhood
the dry brush   the orchards speckled with frostbite
          that told me   home was near
i cried   i drove faster

moments i would mishandle a chore,
like raking leaves, i was sometimes told
*you do everything backwards. you can't do
anything right.* once, in music class while playing
the violin i panicked—fell off notes & swore
the class was laughing at me. i remember
wanting to quit. i kept all my songs
in a shoe box underneath my bed.
i didn't need the world.

i am common as sky. i don't see myself
through other's eyes, or if i do, i dress
the glimmers differently. i rewrite
the same sentence until it rings. i hold
language better than people. my parents shelve
their stories—believe they're unimportant.
i never show them what i've written. my father
struggles to read. poems are the words i put around
the truth. i am still trying to get this right.

morning rose like a quiver of flutes. from my room:
a flagpole, a field of goldenrod, the mountains. i heard
door latches in the hallway click into place. i found you
kneeling at your bedside singing into the sheets, light splayed
on the floor. i lay on a couch playing a thumb piano.
you said that every time you looked out the window
you watched me wading into the flower fields unsure
if i would return. in the evening we stood at the edge
of a landscape & i wanted to bottle the dying light. you spoke
of your brother—the duty to family. being a firstborn,
i nodded. in that silence i could hear my own blood whistle—
so thin & distant from the soil where i stood. on the porch
you asked *who do you sing for?* & i didn't have an answer.
you said *i sing for the dead*—then looked at me—*you do too.*

SUEÑO

i walk into my father's room & my mother stands,
        her back turned to me, wearing

     a dull turquoise bathrobe. i wrap my arms
around her & cry *he never admits*

         he hurts until the day he burst open
     like a rusted water pipe & the floor

was bloated on his breaking & i relearned
        what grief sounds like as it splinters

   through a person. in my brother's room
the television is on & his bed is unmade.

       in my sister's room hang
   her dolls & baby pictures.

she is the amber
       my father's love falls into.

   i snap my fingers next to my ear
to try & wake myself. when it does

not work, for a moment i believe
      it is true—all of us here together

   though we cannot look each other in the face.
when i did wake i had to remind myself

of the new furniture that would not know
      our shape. the empty beds. a dinner table

that no one sat at or prayed over.
   i watched my father pull out all the floorboards

    & cover the ground in cold tile. i said
nothing when he coated the walls white, painting over

an outline where a photograph of my mother hung.

PORTRAIT OF MY YOUNGER BROTHER
WITH BIRDS

in a plaza an elderly lady feeds seed to pigeons. behind her,
a church fills the air with bells. the church's statues look over
everyone & i think at any moment they'll come to life. my brother
watches pigeons from behind a tree, then runs at them & the birds
scatter into the sky the way he imagines a spirit does—dormant in
its cage & then in an instant splintering its way out of bone in a
whirlwind of feathers. once, he wished mr. jackson could be his
father for the way he held his sons. that summer, mr. jackson leapt
off a bridge over the freeway & became a statue sitting inside my
brother's heart. the necklace bouncing against my brother's chest
holds a grain of rice with his name written on it. i wear one too.
our names, our grief—small & delicate. a common soaked grain.
my brother runs & the older lady chases after him. her hands slice
the air. *pinche niño!* he flails his arms as though somewhere tucked
deep inside his body he can find feathers, follow the birds into the sky
& come to perch on a shoulder carved from marble. on a figure
so docile even the most timid creatures lay themselves down inside
its stone hands.

I'M TOLD MY YOUNGER SIBLINGS
LOOK UP TO ME

& i don't know why they would. they don't know
about the faith i built from loss. how i once kissed a mouth
because it would dissolve in the dawn either way.

that i uprooted a forest to sculpt a band of wild horses—
blew smoke into their wooden nostrils. watched
as they stampeded over a town—their hooves pounding into

the soil. that i killed a thing solely to have the part
of its body that i could make music out of. i've been selfish
enough to climb into a song & not come back. i let

dust collect until it suffocates. i left the people
who loved me best to kneel at a stream—watched trout push
against the water, their muscles taut. i failed to catch

even one. i carved the face of someone no longer alive into
the sky so that i did not grieve alone. i plucked the moon. peeled
its rind. as the world turned in the dark, i filled myself on its pulp.

what moves oxygen
through your body.
who you carry inside.
fist-sized muscle clenching

the beloved's letter. the voice
you would follow over
any mountain. a love
that is all possessive adjectives.

the one who pulls the dust-
covered melodies out of you.
who plants a kiss
in the crease of your palm.

the small brick house in the valley.
the one who you hold tighter.
who brings out the jealous daggers
in the blood. the one who every song

must be about. who after all
the breaking you would still return to.
the face that lies at the end
of everything used to forget.

MAMÁ CHELO STANDS AT THE
CONCRETE WASHBOARD

& lays out papá sabino's shirt
along the ridges. turns
   on the faucet & a small river
falls out. fills

   a plastic bowl with water
& pours it over
   the cloth. yesterday he slit
a pig's throat & fed

   his children & nietos,
but the blood stained his sleeve.
   she takes a bar of soap
& rubs the cotton against

   the concrete until the life
of last night's meal comes
   out. she squeezes the damp shirt
& the water hiding in it runs

   into the mouth at the end
of the washboard. she hangs
   the shirt on a clothesline
in the sun. the wind runs through it.

   it smells of rosemary.

PIECING INHERITANCE

my mother tells me that as children, she & her siblings

would often catch a beating from my mamá chelo.

unos buenos madrazos—whether for talking back

or for quarrelling among themselves. she says that once

while mamá chelo helped braid her hair, she sassed,

god amá, times are different now. mamá chelo struck her, yanked

her hair & shouted *don't say that! times are the same then*

as they are now! my mom laughs when she recalls these stories.

//

growing up, my parents beat me
for doing pendejadas.
my mother struck me for slipping
on wet linoleum freshly mopped,
after she had warned me not to.
my father hit me when he found
me in the living room, a sugared
child running in circles & shouting—
he was afraid i'd gone mad.
he wanted to knock sense back
into me. when i was small, my mother
left me in the care of my tía rosa
while she went to work.
when my mother came home,
she found me alone on her bed
facedown & crying low. she asked
tía rosa what had happened
& she replied *i don't know.*

//

my mom says that papá sabino never laid a hand

on her or any of her siblings—except for one instance.

tío primo, after fighting with my mother, said he was leaving

home for good. *oh really?* mamá chelo asked. she called out

to papá sabino, *viejo, this child says he's leaving home.*

he replied, *is that so?* & unbuckled his belt.

my mom says she didn't see it happen, but she heard

the belt lash skin & her brother's cries—*perdóname papá.*

//

when i was a hot-
mouthed adolescent,
my mother slapped me

across the face
for talking back.
i recall most

how still i was
the moment after.
i held my hand

to my face & cried.
never speak
to me like that again.

there was no bruise
or blood, but i felt
something break.

//

i'm trying to say something about fear
& am failing. i'm trying to say that i've learned
fear from the people who fed me. that perhaps
because they knew no other way & panicked,
they believed fear a good instructor for manners
& caution. i'm trying to say that sometimes, the fear
planted & sitting in one body is planted inside another.
that this moment is carried across a lineage until
we can't remember who handed us this gnarled
tradition. i'm trying to say that anger is often fear
with its eyes closed. that i watched my father in a fury
whip a horse again & again for its unruliness. that later,
when i placed my hand on the horse's body, it flinched
at my touch. its breathing measured & labored—
each muscle still & tense. i'm trying to talk
about my first young love. that i watched
the anger & shouting inside her family & said
nothing. that she threw a framed portrait of her parents
against the wall & left glass in the carpet.
during that moment i ran inside myself—
i wanted to vanish. to be neither heard
nor seen—it was all i knew of safety.

into a pool & laugh in disbelief.
—you never knew he could swim.
he treads water, grins & asks,
no supiste que podía nadar?
he tells you that in his youth
on the warm days leading up to summer
he & some other boys would run down
to the river after school, strip,
then jump into the water.
i haven't swam much since then,
he says, *but i still remember.*
it seems too gentle for him—
someone who you believe
or who would have you believe
he was only ever a child of toil.
but it's also true
that there were moments
to dance, to sing, to swim.
you imagine that river glistening—
your father, a small child, learning
how to let water hold him.
about his life you know only parts—
the little he's told you,
the stories you hear from family.
like when he set out
on a pilgrimage from his small town
to the basílica in méxico city
& prayed to the virgen de guadalupe
to cure his ailing father.
or when, one night at a dance hall,
he saw your mother for the first time
& after they danced, he gave her
a note with his name & number.
how can you ask the people
you love about their life?
you can only wade

through hushed water,
finding pieces of a portrait
imperfect & blue—whispering
at the bottom
of memory.

WELD

from inside your room
you heard your father
alone in his shed

striking red-hot iron—
each clang piercing
the blaring radio.

he struggled to let anyone in
—even your mother.
about his marriage & fatherhood

he'd say *maybe i made mistakes*
—i couldn't always be there
but i wasn't a bum or a drunk

—i wasn't as bad as i could've been.
all you could ever share
with him was work & sweat.

when you were young he placed
a scrap of metal in your hand
& closed your small fingers

around it. you named it
doubt, named it silence.
you spend your life

trying to undo your fist
to weld cold metal
into something of joy.

something soft & curved—
a horn, a wind chime,
a silver whistle—

something for song.

you hear a part of your life on the opposite
side of the river. you don't know when it found

its way outside of you—like when one
of the smaller nesting days inside vanishes for good—

you can never have it again, but make peace
with the fact. you say to yourself *that was then.*

you don't think about crossing the river. you know
the current is strong enough to pummel you—

the past is like that. instead, for a moment, you look
for the people across the water & they can't see or hear

you, of course, but you can make out fireflies
dancing—you can hear people singing.

& it's only until the near end of the song
that you notice you've been mouthing every single word.

ORIGIN MYTH

the child who never stopped running grew
up to become the wind—left behind their body

& its boulders to blow ships across the water & spin
the lone weathervane on the barn. the girl who spent

days making birds from lightning & clay to feel less
alone became a god—there were a thousand hands

reaching to her for an answer, but never her palms.
the boy whose grief was too big for his body became

the ocean—everyone knew the shape of his sorrow & we all
thrashed our way out of him after breaking the glass-like

surface. the baby born with holes in their skin let the breeze
weave through their body, let a hundred notes rise into

the air & grew up to be a song. the child so desperate
to be near those far away reached into the sky & became

smoke. the child who continued to love unbittered
by this world became the sun. he rises every morning to cover

the earth in light & look how he has never dimmed.